TROMBONE

The **BIG BOOK** of

trombone songs

AVAILABLE FOR:
Flute, Clarinet, Alto Sax, Tenor Sax, Trumpet,
Horn, Trombone, Violin, Viola, and Cello

ISBN 978-1-4234-2669-1

Visit Hal Leonard Online at
www.halleonard.com

Contact Us:
Hal Leonard
7777 West Bluemound Road
Milwaukee, WI 53213
Email: info@halleonard.com

In Europe contact:
Hal Leonard Europe Limited
Distribution Centre, Newmarket Road
Bury St Edmunds, Suffolk, IP33 3YB
Email: info@halleonardeurope.com

In Australia contact:
Hal Leonard Australia Pty. Ltd.
4 Lentara Court
Cheltenham, Victoria, 3192 Australia
Email: info@halleonard.com.au

CONTENTS

4 All My Loving
5 All the Small Things
6 Alley Cat
8 America
7 Another One Bites the Dust
10 Any Dream Will Do
12 Bad Day
14 Barely Breathing
11 Be True to Your School
16 (It's A) Beautiful Morning
17 Beauty and the Beast
18 Beyond the Sea
19 Blackbird
20 Blue Suede Shoes
21 Boogie Woogie Bugle Boy
22 The Brady Bunch
24 Breaking Free
23 Butterfly Kisses
26 Cabaret
27 California Dreamin'
28 Candle in the Wind
29 Chim Chim Cher-ee
30 Clocks
31 (They Long to Be) Close to You
32 Colors of the Wind
33 Come Fly with Me
34 Copacabana (At the Copa)
35 Do-Re-Mi
36 Do Wah Diddy Diddy
37 (Sittin' On) The Dock of the Bay
38 Don't Be Cruel (To a Heart That's True)
39 Don't Let the Sun Go Down on Me
40 Don't Speak
42 Drift Away
43 Duke of Earl
44 Theme from E.T. (The Extra-Terrestrial)
45 Edelweiss
46 Every Breath You Take
47 Everything Is Beautiful
48 Fallin'
50 Fields of Gold
51 Fly Like an Eagle
52 For Once in My Life
53 Forever Young
54 Fun, Fun, Fun
55 The Girl from Ipanema (Garôta de Ipanema)
56 God Bless the U.S.A.
57 Gonna Build a Mountain
58 Goodbye Yellow Brick Road
59 Green Green Grass of Home
60 Happy Days
61 Have I Told You Lately
62 Heart and Soul
64 Here Without You
63 Hogan's Heroes March
66 I Dreamed a Dream
67 I Heard It Through the Grapevine
68 I Say a Little Prayer
69 I Whistle a Happy Tune
70 I Will Remember You
71 I Write the Songs
72 I'm Popeye the Sailor Man
73 If I Ever Lose My Faith in You
74 Imagine
75 It's My Life

76 It's Still Rock and Roll to Me
77 Jailhouse Rock
78 Joy to the World
79 Jump, Jive an' Wail
80 Kansas City
81 Kokomo
82 Let 'Em In
83 Let's Stay Together
84 Like a Rock
86 Livin' La Vida Loca
87 Love and Marriage
88 Love Story
89 Maggie May
90 Making Our Dreams Come True
91 Maybe I'm Amazed
92 Michelle
93 Mickey Mouse March
94 Mission: Impossible Theme
95 Mister Sandman
96 Moon River
97 My Heart Will Go On (Love Theme from 'Titanic')
98 My Way
99 Na Na Hey Hey Kiss Him Goodbye
100 On Broadway
101 Peppermint Twist
102 Pocketful of Miracles
103 Puff the Magic Dragon
104 Put Your Hand in the Hand
105 Quiet Nights of Quiet Stars (Corcovado)
106 Rock Around the Clock
107 Rock with You
108 Satin Doll
109 Save the Best for Last
110 Theme from "Schindler's List"
111 She Will Be Loved
112 Sing
113 So Long, Farewell
114 Somewhere Out There
115 Spanish Flea
116 Stacy's Mom
118 Sunrise, Sunset
119 Take My Breath Away (Love Theme)
120 That's Amoré (That's Love)
121 This Land Is Your Land
122 Those Were the Days
124 A Thousand Miles
123 Time After Time
126 Tomorrow
127 Top of the World
128 Twist and Shout
129 Unchained Melody
130 Under the Boardwalk
131 United We Stand
132 The Way You Move
133 We Are the World
134 We Belong Together
136 What the World Needs Now Is Love
137 With a Little Help from My Friends
138 Wonderful Tonight
139 Wooly Bully
140 Yellow Submarine
141 You Are the Sunshine of My Life
142 You Raise Me Up
143 You've Got a Friend
144 Zip-A-Dee-Doo-Dah

ALL MY LOVING
from A HARD DAY'S NIGHT

TROMBONE

Words and Music by JOHN LENNON
and PAUL McCARTNEY

ALL THE SMALL THINGS

TROMBONE

Words and Music by TOM DE LONGE and MARK HOPPUS

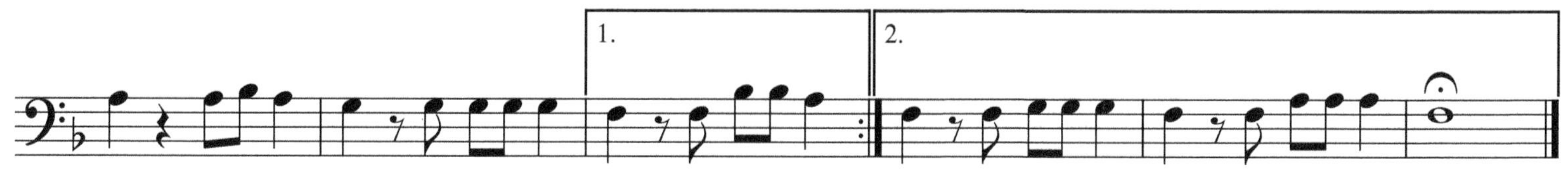

ALLEY CAT

TROMBONE

By FRANK BJORN

ANOTHER ONE BITES THE DUST

TROMBONE

Words and Music by
JOHN DEACON

Steady Rock

To Coda

1.

2.

D.C. al Coda

CODA

AMERICA

from the Motion Picture THE JAZZ SINGER

TROMBONE

Words and Music by
NEIL DIAMOND

Moderately

1.

2.

small notes optional

1.
2.

ANY DREAM WILL DO

from JOSEPH AND THE AMAZING TECHNICOLOR® DREAMCOAT

TROMBONE

Music by ANDREW LLOYD WEBBER
Lyrics by TIM RICE

BE TRUE TO YOUR SCHOOL

TROMBONE

Words and Music by BRIAN WILSON
and MIKE LOVE

BAD DAY

TROMBONE

Words and Music by
DANIEL POWTER

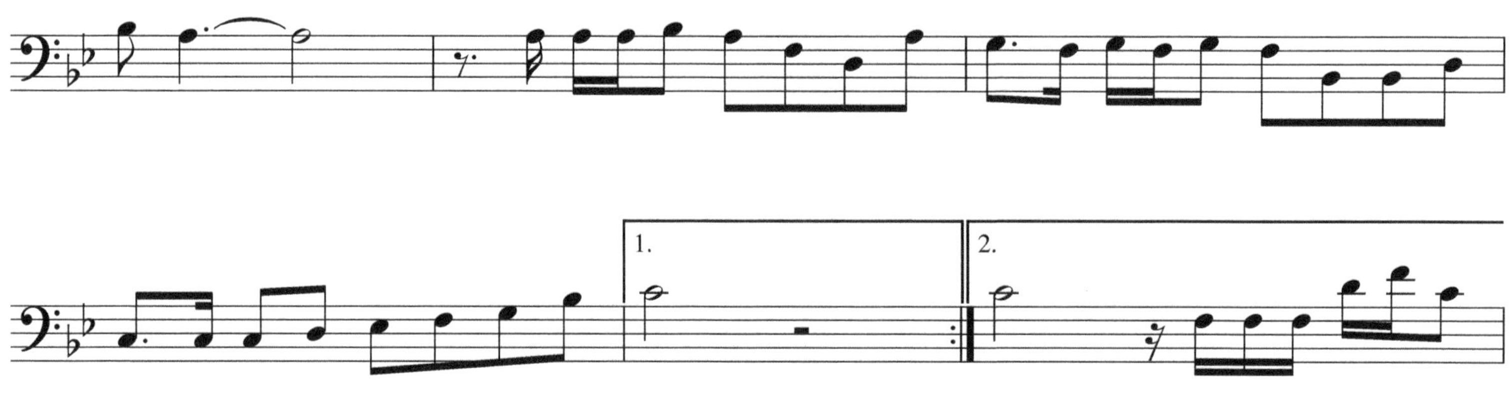

D.S. al Coda
CODA

BARELY BREATHING

TROMBONE

Words and Music by
DUNCAN SHEIK

Moderately

1.
2., 3.
3
3
To Coda
3
D.S. al Coda
CODA

(It's A)
BEAUTIFUL MORNING

TROMBONE

Words and Music by FELIX CAVALIERE
and EDWARD BRIGATI, JR.

BEAUTY AND THE BEAST

from Walt Disney's BEAUTY AND THE BEAST

TROMBONE

Lyrics by HOWARD ASHMAN
Music by ALAN MENKEN

BEYOND THE SEA

TROMBONE

Words and Music by CHARLES TRENET,
ALBERT LASRY and JACK LAWRENCE

BLACKBIRD

TROMBONE

Words and Music by JOHN LENNON
and PAUL McCARTNEY

BLUE SUEDE SHOES

TROMBONE

Words and Music by
CARL LEE PERKINS

BOOGIE WOOGIE BUGLE BOY

from BUCK PRIVATES

TROMBONE

Words and Music by DON RAYE
and HUGHIE PRINCE

THE BRADY BUNCH

Theme from the Paramount Television Series THE BRADY BUNCH

TROMBONE

Words and Music by SHERWOOD SCHWARTZ
and FRANK DEVOL

BUTTERFLY KISSES

TROMBONE

Words and Music by BOB CARLISLE
and RANDY THOMAS

BREAKING FREE

from the Disney Channel Original Movie HIGH SCHOOL MUSICAL

TROMBONE

Words and Music by
JAMIE HOUSTON

CABARET

from the Musical CABARET

TROMBONE

Words by FRED EBB
Music by JOHN KANDER

CALIFORNIA DREAMIN'

TROMBONE

Words and Music by JOHN PHILLIPS
and MICHELLE PHILLIPS

CANDLE IN THE WIND

TROMBONE

Words and Music by ELTON JOHN
and BERNIE TAUPIN

CHIM CHIM CHER-EE

from Walt Disney's MARY POPPINS

TROMBONE

Words and Music by RICHARD M. SHERMAN
and ROBERT B. SHERMAN

Lightly, with gusto

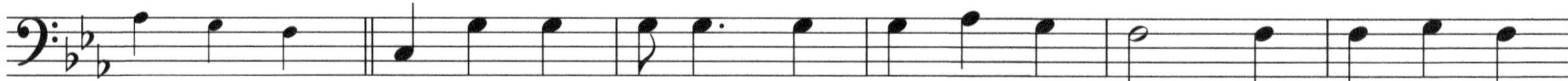

CLOCKS

TROMBONE

Words and Music by GUY BERRYMAN, JON BUCKLAND, WILL CHAMPION and CHRIS MARTIN

(They Long to Be)

CLOSE TO YOU

TROMBONE

Lyric by HAL DAVID
Music by BURT BACHARACH

COLORS OF THE WIND

from Walt Disney's POCAHONTAS

TROMBONE

Music by ALAN MENKEN
Lyrics by STEPHEN SCHWARTZ

COME FLY WITH ME

TROMBONE

Words by SAMMY CAHN
Music by JAMES VAN HEUSEN

COPACABANA
(At the Copa)
from Barry Manilow's COPACABANA

TROMBONE

Music by BARRY MANILOW
Lyric by BRUCE SUSSMAN and JACK FELDMAN

DO-RE-MI

from THE SOUND OF MUSIC

TROMBONE

Lyrics by OSCAR HAMMERSTEIN II
Music by RICHARD RODGERS

Lively

1.

2.

DO WAH DIDDY DIDDY

TROMBONE

Words and Music by JEFF BARRY
and ELLIE GREENWICH

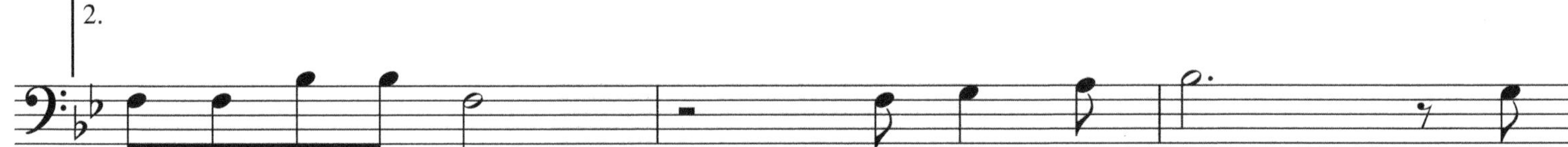

(Sittin' On)

THE DOCK OF THE BAY

TROMBONE

Words and Music by STEVE CROPPER
and OTIS REDDING

DON'T BE CRUEL
(To a Heart That's True)

TROMBONE

Words and Music by OTIS BLACKWELL
and ELVIS PRESLEY

Medium bright (♫ = ♩♪ triplet)

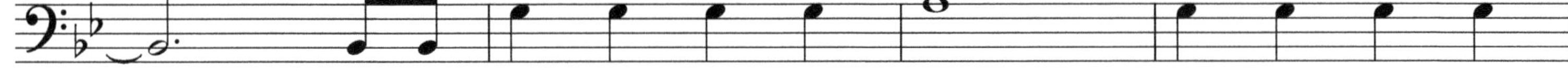

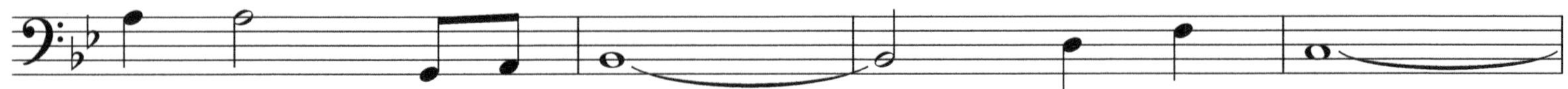

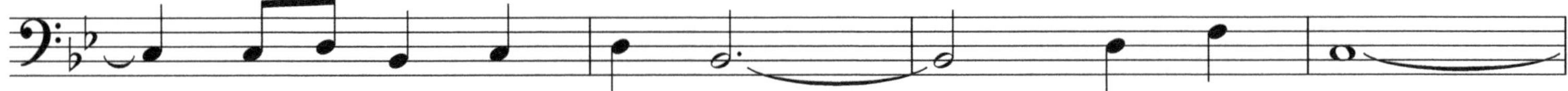

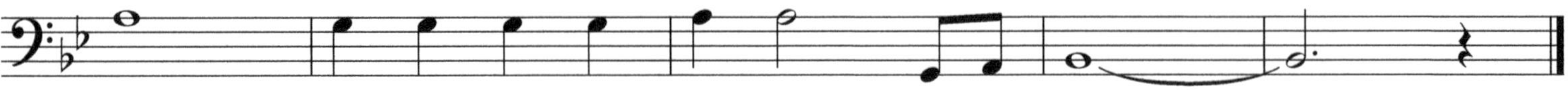

DON'T LET THE SUN GO DOWN ON ME

TROMBONE

Words and Music by ELTON JOHN
and BERNIE TAUPIN

Slow Rock

DON'T SPEAK

TROMBONE

Words and Music by ERIC STEFANI
and GWEN STEFANI

D.S. al Coda
CODA
3
small notes optional

DRIFT AWAY

TROMBONE

Words and Music by
MENTOR WILLIAMS

Moderately fast

To Coda

1.

2.

D.C. al Coda

CODA

DUKE OF EARL

TROMBONE

Words and Music by EARL EDWARDS,
EUGENE DIXON and BERNICE WILLIAMS

THEME FROM E.T. (THE EXTRA-TERRESTRIAL)

from the Universal Picture E.T. (THE EXTRA-TERRESTRIAL)

TROMBONE

Music by
JOHN WILLIAMS

EDELWEISS

from THE SOUND OF MUSIC

TROMBONE

Lyrics by OSCAR HAMMERSTEIN II
Music by RICHARD RODGERS

EVERY BREATH YOU TAKE

TROMBONE

Music and Lyrics by
STING

EVERYTHING IS BEAUTIFUL

TROMBONE

Words and Music by
RAY STEVENS

Moderately fast

1. 2.

FALLIN'

TROMBONE

Words and Music by
ALICIA KEYS

1., 2.
3.

FIELDS OF GOLD

TROMBONE

Music and Lyrics by
STING

FLY LIKE AN EAGLE

TROMBONE

Words and Music by
STEVE MILLER

FOR ONCE IN MY LIFE

TROMBONE

Words by RONALD MILLER
Music by ORLANDO MURDEN

FOREVER YOUNG

TROMBONE

Words and Music by ROD STEWART, JIM CREGAN, KEVIN SAVIGAR and BOB DYLAN

FUN, FUN, FUN

TROMBONE

Words and Music by BRIAN WILSON
and MIKE LOVE

Bright Rock

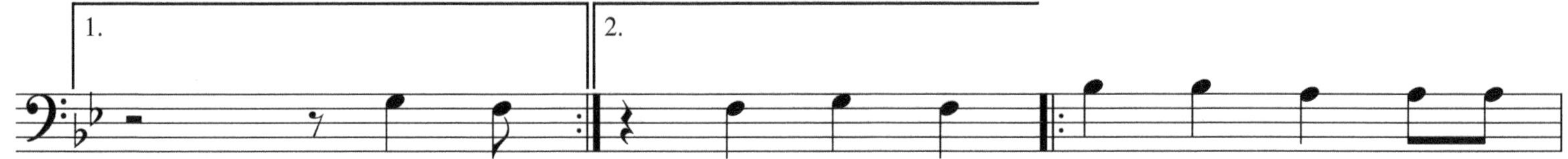

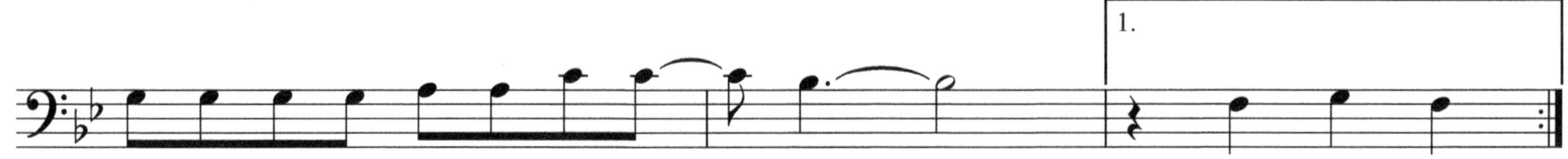

THE GIRL FROM IPANEMA

(Garôta de Ipanema)

TROMBONE

Music by ANTONIO CARLOS JOBIM
English Words by NORMAN GIMBEL
Original Words by VINICIUS DE MORAES

GOD BLESS THE U.S.A

TROMBONE

Words and Music by
LEE GREENWOOD

GONNA BUILD A MOUNTAIN

from the Musical Production STOP THE WORLD – I WANT TO GET OFF

TROMBONE

Words and Music by LESLIE BRICUSSE
and ANTHONY NEWLEY

Moderately bright

GOODBYE YELLOW BRICK ROAD

TROMBONE

Words and Music by ELTON JOHN
and BERNIE TAUPIN

Moderately slow, in 2

GREEN GREEN GRASS OF HOME

TROMBONE

Words and Music by
CURLY PUTMAN

HAPPY DAYS

Theme from the Paramount Television Series HAPPY DAYS

TROMBONE

Words by NORMAN GIMBEL
Music by CHARLES FOX

HAVE I TOLD YOU LATELY

TROMBONE

Words and Music by
VAN MORRISON

HEART AND SOUL

from the Paramount Short Subject A SONG IS BORN

TROMBONE

Words by FRANK LOESSER
Music by HOAGY CARMICHAEL

HOGAN'S HEROES MARCH

from the Television Series HOGAN'S HEROES

TROMBONE

By JERRY FIELDING

HERE WITHOUT YOU

TROMBONE

Words and Music by MATT ROBERTS,
BRAD ARNOLD, CHRISTOPHER HENDERSON
and ROBERT HARRELL

1.
2.
4

I DREAMED A DREAM

from LES MISÉRABLES

TROMBONE

Music by CLAUDE-MICHEL SCHÖNBERG
Lyrics by ALAIN BOUBLIL, JEAN-MARC NATEL
and HERBERT KRETZMER

I HEARD IT THROUGH THE GRAPEVINE

TROMBONE

Words and Music by NORMAN J. WHITFIELD
and BARRETT STRONG

I SAY A LITTLE PRAYER

TROMBONE

Lyric by HAL DAVID
Music by BURT BACHARACH

I WHISTLE A HAPPY TUNE

from THE KING AND I

TROMBONE

Lyrics by OSCAR HAMMERSTEIN II
Music by RICHARD RODGERS

Brightly

I WILL REMEMBER YOU

Theme from THE BROTHERS McMULLEN

TROMBONE

Words and Music by SARAH McLACHLAN,
SEAMUS EGAN and DAVE MERENDA

I WRITE THE SONGS

TROMBONE

Words and Music by
BRUCE JOHNSTON

Slow Ballad

1.

2.

I'M POPEYE THE SAILOR MAN

Theme from the Paramount Cartoon POPEYE THE SAILOR

TROMBONE

Words and Music by
SAMMY LERNER

IF I EVER LOSE MY FAITH IN YOU

TROMBONE

Music and Lyrics by
STING

IMAGINE

TROMBONE

Words and Music by
JOHN LENNON

Medium slow

1.

2.

IT'S MY LIFE

TROMBONE

Words and Music by JON BON JOVI, RICHARD SAMBORA and MARTIN SANDBERG

IT'S STILL ROCK AND ROLL TO ME

TROMBONE

Words and Music by
BILLY JOEL

JAILHOUSE ROCK

TROMBONE

Words and Music by JERRY LEIBER
and MIKE STOLLER

JOY TO THE WORLD

TROMBONE

Words and Music by
HOYT AXTON

JUMP, JIVE AN' WAIL

TROMBONE

Words and Music by
LOUIS PRIMA

KANSAS CITY

TROMBONE

Words and Music by JERRY LEIBER and MIKE STOLLER

KOKOMO

from the Motion Picture COCKTAIL

TROMBONE

Words and Music by MIKE LOVE, TERRY MELCHER, JOHN PHILLIPS and SCOTT McKENZIE

LET 'EM IN

TROMBONE

Words and Music by
PAUL and LINDA McCARTNEY

Moderately

LET'S STAY TOGETHER

TROMBONE

Words and Music by AL GREEN,
WILLIE MITCHELL and AL JACKSON, JR.

LIKE A ROCK

TROMBONE

Words and Music by
BOB SEGER

Moderately

To Coda

D.S. al Coda
CODA

LIVIN' LA VIDA LOCA

TROMBONE

Words and Music by ROBI ROSA and DESMOND CHILD

Fast, with a steady beat

1. 2.

LOVE AND MARRIAGE

TROMBONE

Words by SAMMY CAHN
Music by JAMES VAN HEUSEN

LOVE STORY

Theme from the Paramount Picture LOVE STORY

TROMBONE

Music by FRANCIS LAI

MAGGIE MAY

TROMBONE

Words and Music by ROD STEWART
and MARTIN QUITTENTON

MAKING OUR DREAMS COME TRUE

Theme from the Paramount Television Series LAVERNE AND SHIRLEY

TROMBONE

Words by NORMAN GIMBEL
Music by CHARLES FOX

MAYBE I'M AMAZED

TROMBONE

Words and Music by
PAUL McCARTNEY

MICHELLE

TROMBONE

Words and Music by JOHN LENNON
and PAUL McCARTNEY

MICKEY MOUSE MARCH

from Walt Disney's THE MICKEY MOUSE CLUB

TROMBONE

Words and Music by
JIMMIE DODD

MISSION: IMPOSSIBLE THEME

From the Paramount Television Series MISSION: IMPOSSIBLE

TROMBONE

By LALO SCHIFRIN

MISTER SANDMAN

TROMBONE

Lyric and Music by
PAT BALLARD

MOON RIVER

from the Paramount Picture BREAKFAST AT TIFFANY'S

TROMBONE

Words by JOHNNY MERCER
Music by HENRY MANCINI

MY HEART WILL GO ON

(Love Theme from 'Titanic')
from the Paramount and Twentieth Century Fox Motion Picture TITANIC

TROMBONE

Music by JAMES HORNER
Lyric by WILL JENNINGS

MY WAY

TROMBONE

English Words by PAUL ANKA
Original French Words by GILLES THIBAULT
Music by JACQUES REVAUX and CLAUDE FRANCOIS

NA NA HEY HEY KISS HIM GOODBYE

TROMBONE

Words and Music by ARTHUR FRASHUER DALE,
PAUL ROGER LEKA and GARY CARLA

ON BROADWAY

TROMBONE

Words and Music by BARRY MANN,
CYNTHIA WEIL, MIKE STOLLER and JERRY LEIBER

PEPPERMINT TWIST

TROMBONE

Words and Music by JOSEPH DiNICOLA
and HENRY GLOVER

POCKETFUL OF MIRACLES

TROMBONE

Words by SAMMY CAHN
Music by JAMES VAN HEUSEN

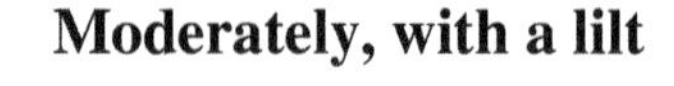

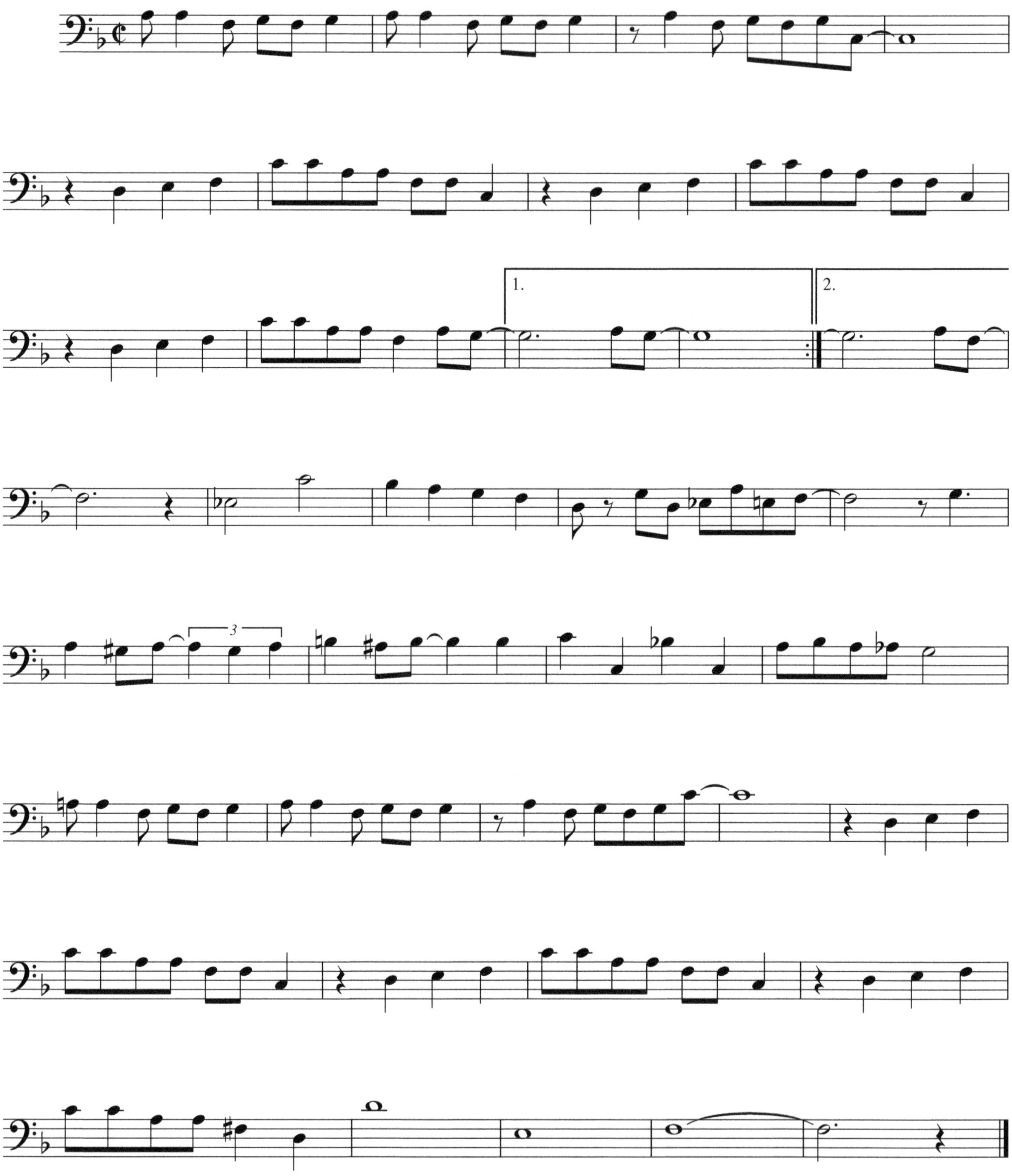

1.

2.

3

PUFF THE MAGIC DRAGON

TROMBONE

Words and Music by LENNY LIPTON
and PETER YARROW

PUT YOUR HAND IN THE HAND

TROMBONE

Words and Music by
GENE MacLELLAN

QUIET NIGHTS OF QUIET STARS

(Corcovado)

TROMBONE

English Words by GENE LEES
Original Words and Music by ANTONIO CARLOS JOBIM

Moderately slow

ROCK AROUND THE CLOCK

TROMBONE

Words and Music by MAX C. FREEDMAN
and JIMMY DeKNIGHT

ROCK WITH YOU

TROMBONE

Words and Music by
ROD TEMPERTON

SATIN DOLL

TROMBONE

By DUKE ELLINGTON

SAVE THE BEST FOR LAST

TROMBONE

Words and Music by PHIL GALDSTON,
JON LIND and WENDY WALDMAN

THEME FROM "SCHINDLER'S LIST"

from the Universal Motion Picture SCHINDLER'S LIST

TROMBONE

Music by JOHN WILLIAMS

SHE WILL BE LOVED

TROMBONE

Words and Music by ADAM LEVINE
and JAMES VALENTINE

Moderately

To Coda

1.

2.

CODA

D.S. al Coda

Play 3 times

SING
from SESAME STREET

TROMBONE

Words and Music by
JOE RAPOSO

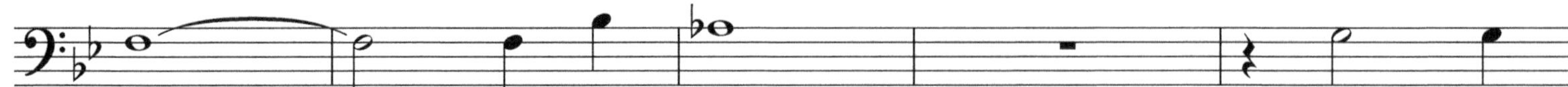

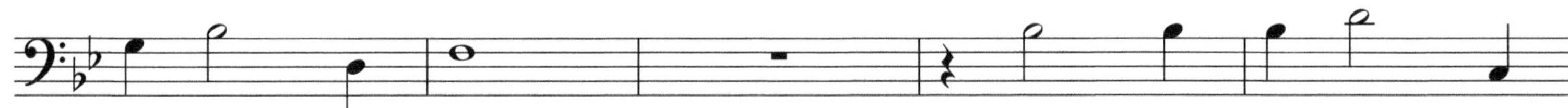

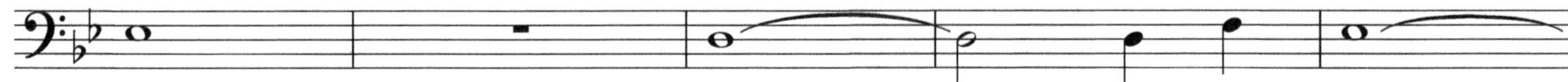

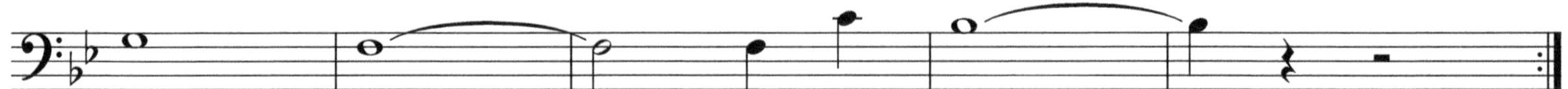

SO LONG, FAREWELL
from THE SOUND OF MUSIC

TROMBONE

Lyrics by OSCAR HAMMERSTEIN II
Music by RICHARD RODGERS

Moderately

small notes optional

1., 2.

3.

Slower

SOMEWHERE OUT THERE

from AN AMERICAN TAIL

TROMBONE

Music by BARRY MANN and JAMES HORNER
Lyric by CYNTHIA WEIL

SPANISH FLEA

TROMBONE

Words and Music by
JULIUS WECHTER

STACY'S MOM

TROMBONE

Words and Music by CHRIS COLLINGWOOD
and ADAM SCHLESINGER

Medium Rock

SUNRISE, SUNSET

from the Musical FIDDLER ON THE ROOF

TROMBONE

Words by SHELDON HARNICK
Music by JERRY BOCK

TAKE MY BREATH AWAY

(Love Theme)
from the Paramount Picture TOP GUN

TROMBONE

Words and Music by GIORGIO MORODER
and TOM WHITLOCK

Moderately slow

THAT'S AMORÉ

(That's Love)

from the Paramount Picture THE CADDY

TROMBONE

Words by JACK BROOKS
Music by HARRY WARREN

Moderately

1.

2.

THIS LAND IS YOUR LAND

TROMBONE

Words and Music by
WOODY GUTHRIE

THOSE WERE THE DAYS

TROMBONE

Words and Music by
GENE RASKIN

TIME AFTER TIME

TROMBONE

Words and Music by CYNDI LAUPER
and ROB HYMAN

Moderately fast Rock

A THOUSAND MILES

TROMBONE

Words and Music by
VANESSA CARLTON

Moderately fast

2.
D.C. al Coda
CODA

TOMORROW

from the Musical Production ANNIE

TROMBONE

Lyric by MARTIN CHARNIN
Music by CHARLES STROUSE

TOP OF THE WORLD

TROMBONE

Words and Music by JOHN BETTIS
and RICHARD CARPENTER

TWIST AND SHOUT

TROMBONE

Words and Music by BERT RUSSELL
and PHIL MEDLEY

UNCHAINED MELODY

TROMBONE

Lyric by HY ZARET
Music by ALEX NORTH

UNDER THE BOARDWALK

TROMBONE

Words and Music by ARTIE RESNICK
and KENNY YOUNG

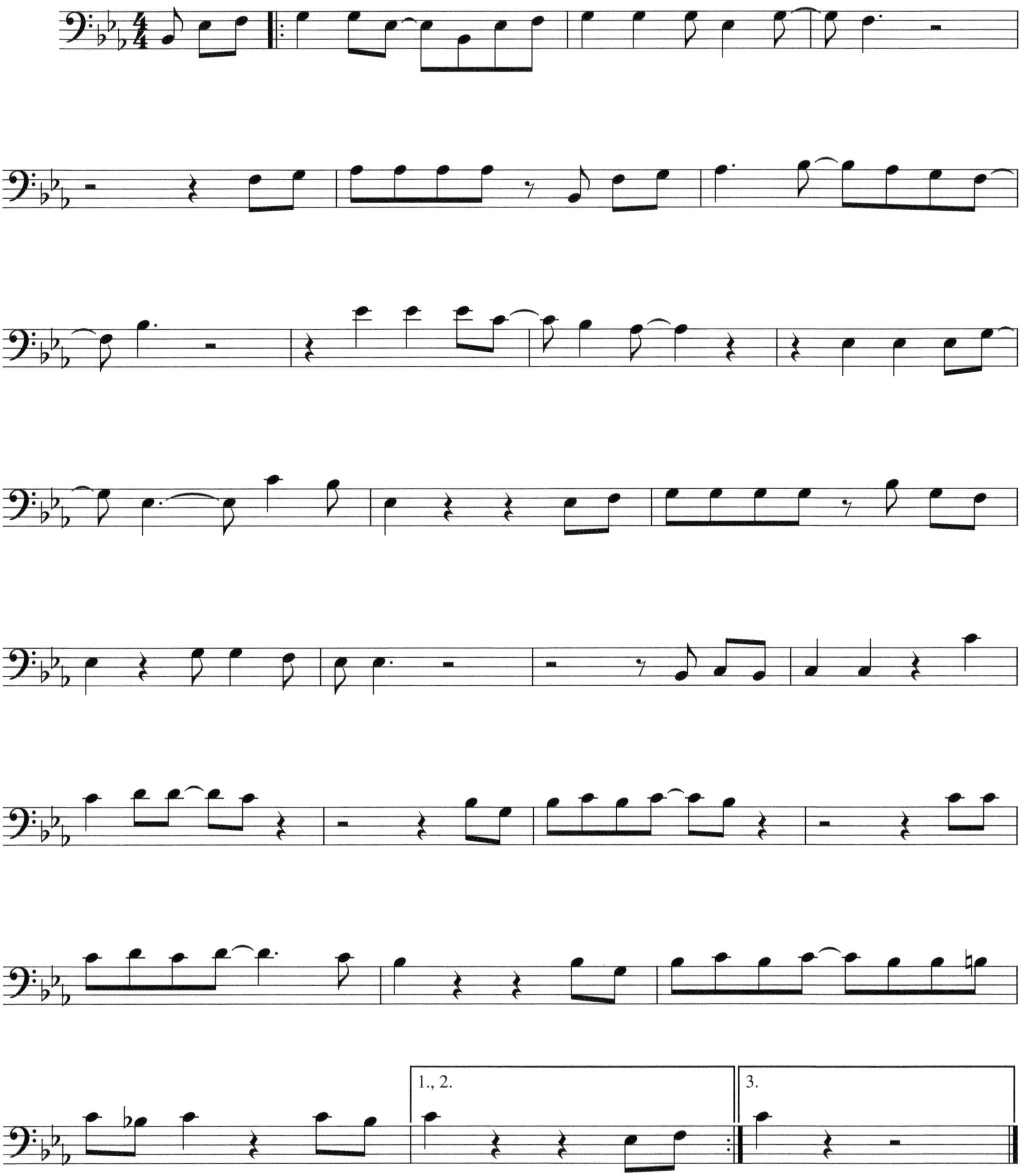

1., 2.

3.

UNITED WE STAND

TROMBONE

Words and Music by ANTHONY TOBY HILLER
and JOHN GOODISON

THE WAY YOU MOVE

TROMBONE

Words and Music by ANTWAN PATTON, PATRICK BROWN and CARLTON MAHONE

Moderate groove

WE ARE THE WORLD

TROMBONE

Words and Music by LIONEL RICHIE
and MICHAEL JACKSON

Moderately slow

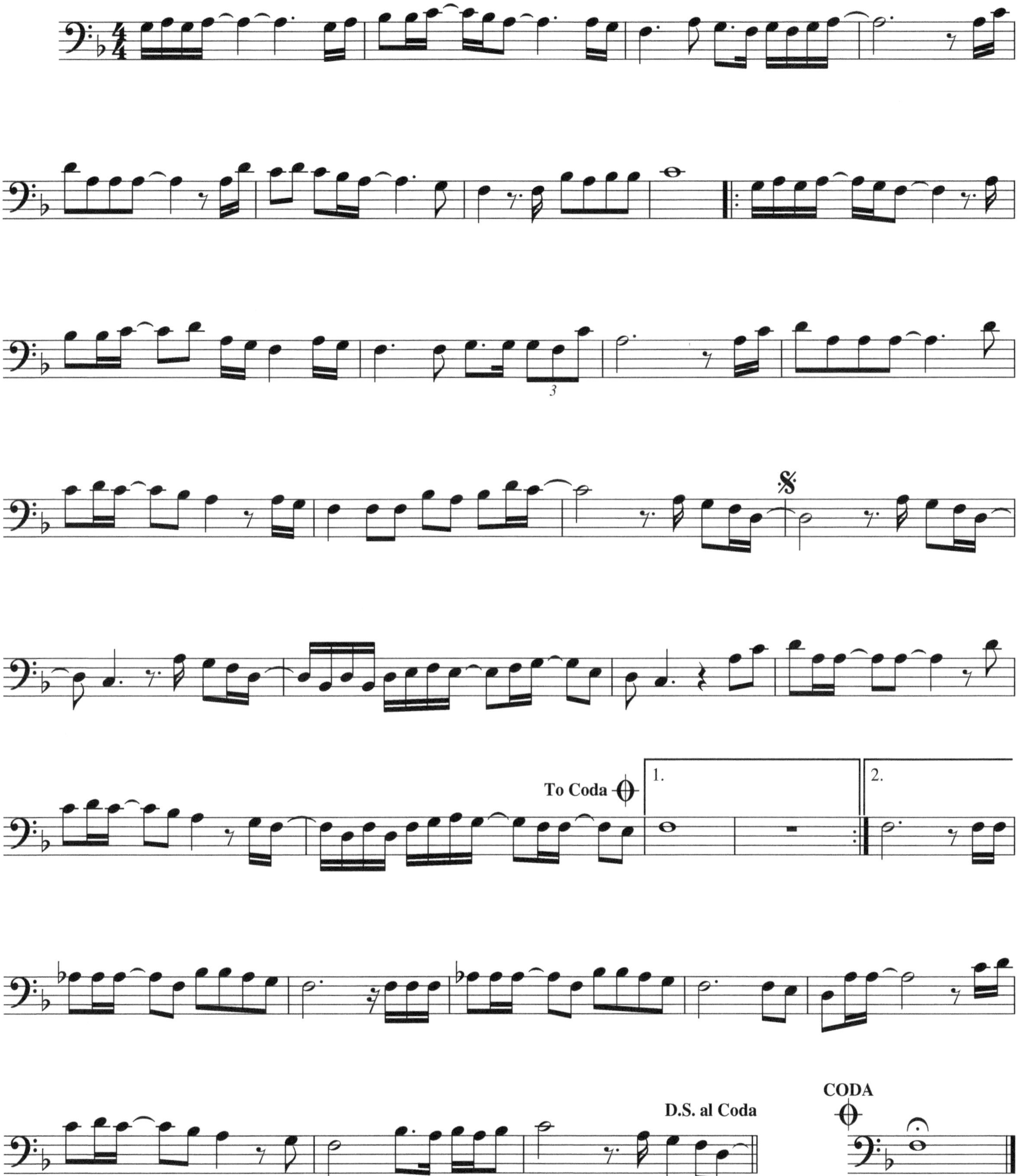

3

𝄋

To Coda

1.

2.

D.S. al Coda

CODA

WE BELONG TOGETHER

TROMBONE

Words and Music by MARIAH CAREY,
JERMAINE DUPRI, MANUEL SEAL, JOHNTA AUSTIN,
DARNELL BRISTOL, KENNETH EDMONDS, SIDNEY JOHNSON,
PATRICK MOTEN, BOBBY WOMACK and SANDRA SULLY

- contains elements of "Two Occasions" by Darnell Bristol, Kenneth Edmonds and Sidney Johnson and "If You Think You're Lonely Now" by Patrick Moten, Bobby Womack and Sandra Sully

To Coda
D.S. al Coda
CODA

WHAT THE WORLD NEEDS NOW IS LOVE

TROMBONE

Lyric by HAL DAVID
Music by BURT BACHARACH

WITH A LITTLE HELP FROM MY FRIENDS

TROMBONE

Words and Music by JOHN LENNON
and PAUL McCARTNEY

WONDERFUL TONIGHT

TROMBONE

Words and Music by
ERIC CLAPTON

WOOLY BULLY

TROMBONE

Words and Music by
DOMINGO SAMUDIO

YELLOW SUBMARINE

TROMBONE

Words and Music by JOHN LENNON
and PAUL McCARTNEY

YOU ARE THE SUNSHINE OF MY LIFE

TROMBONE

Words and Music by
STEVIE WONDER

YOU RAISE ME UP

TROMBONE

Words and Music by BRENDAN GRAHAM
and ROLF LOVLAND

YOU'VE GOT A FRIEND

TROMBONE

Words and Music by
CAROLE KING

Slowly

To Coda

1.

2.

D.S. al Coda

CODA

ZIP-A-DEE-DOO-DAH

from Walt Disney's SONG OF THE SOUTH
from Disneyland and Walt Disney World's SPLASH MOUNTAIN

TROMBONE

Words by RAY GILBERT
Music by ALLIE WRUBEL